**The Apostle Creeds:
A Brief Commentary
by Ps JJ Lim**

Brief Comments © 2013, 2018 by JJ Lim

This edition published in 2018 by
Pilgrim Covenant Church
Singapore

Content

THE APOSTLES' CREED

I. *I believe in God, the Father Almighty, Maker of heaven and earth;*

II. *And in Jesus Christ, His only begotten Son, our Lord;*

III. *Who was conceived by the Holy Ghost, born of the virgin Mary;*

IV. *Suffered under Pontius Pilate; was crucified, dead, and buried: He descended into hell;*

V. *The third day He arose again from the dead;*

VI. *He ascended into heaven, and sitteth at the right hand of God the Father Almighty;*

VII. *From thence He shall come to judge the quick and the dead.*

VIII. *I believe in the Holy Ghost;*

IX. *I believe an holy catholic church: the communion of saints;*

X. *The forgiveness of sins;*

XI. *The resurrection of the body;*

XII. *And the life everlasting. AMEN.*

Comments

This is the most ancient ecumenical creed of the New Testament Church. It is called the Apostles' Creed not because it was written by the apostles. Rather, it is so-called because of its antiquity and its reflection of the main points which the apostles would have emphasised judging from the Gospel accounts. Indeed, it is very possible that some of the statements in its earliest form could have been enumerated by the apostles and their successors as they catechised new converts and covenant children.

There is evidence that the most basic form of this creed was already in use in about AD 200 though there was never any official endorsement by any of the ecumenical councils.

The present form, which is commonly recited in traditional and Continental Reformed Churches, however, dates to the middle of the 7th Century. In particular, the phrase "He descended into hell" in the 4th article was not found in any version prior to A.D. 650, though a version in A.D. 390 refers to Christ descending into Hades or the place of the dead. In any case, certain sectors of Christianity have insisted on the basis of this phrase that Christ actually descended to hell or to what is called the *Limbus Patrium* to preach to the unconverted who died earlier. The Protestant and Reformed Church have generally interpreted the phrase differently. John Calvin, who argues that the phrase must be retained even though it was a late insertion, suggests that by it the church confesses that Christ did not only suffer bodily but spiritually in that He suffered the pains of hell on behalf of the Church while on the Cross (cf. *ICR* 2.16.8). This is taken up in the Heidelberg Catechism, Q. 44: "Why is it added: He descended into Hell?" The answer supplied is: "That in my greatest temptations I may be assured that Christ, my Lord, by

His inexpressible anguish, pains and terrors, which He suffered in His soul on the cross and before, has redeemed me from the anguish and torment of hell." *The Westminster Larger Catechism,* on the other hand, while not denying that Christ suffered the pains of hell for us, observes that the event mentioned in the Creed occurred after the Lord's burial, and therefore, it is a reference to Christ being "under the power of death till the third day" (*WLC* 50).

All other statements in the creed are straightforward and non-controversial. Nevertheless, it will be useful for us to look at them briefly, one article at a time.

Article I:
Of God our Creator

I believe in God, the Father Almighty,
Maker of heaven and earth;

Comments

The Apostles' Creed is seldom used by itself as a unifying confession in today's church because over the centuries many varieties of Christian churches which can claim subscription to it have arisen. We think of Roman Catholics, Eastern Orthodox, Lutherans, Anglicans, Methodist and Presbyterians amongst others. All these churches can claim subscription to it. But "Can two walk together, except they be agreed?" (Amos 3:3). Unity based on the Apostles' Creed today is no real unity. Nevertheless, the Creed contains the basic propositions that every true believer must believe and confess with proper understanding. Faith is a gift of God, but true faith is not empty. True faith is faith in Christ, but Christ does not stand apart from the context of His existence in the Godhead or of the Church and of the blessings He has procured for her. This creed covers these things with very broad strokes in twelve articles.

In the first article, we are given to confess that we, individually, *"believe in God, the Father Almighty, Maker of heaven and earth."* What do we mean by that? At first sight, this seems rather straightforward, but things get a little complicated when we realise that this is the first creed in which the doctrine of the Trinity is asserted, and it is asserted without the clarity of, say, the Athanasian Creed of the 4th century. Nevertheless, as it stands it reflects something of the difficulties that theologians have when they try to reduce the theology of the Scriptures into a few propositions.

With the more developed understanding that we have today, we generally express first our belief that there is only one living and true God and then affirm that there are three persons in the Godhead, the Father, Son and Holy Ghost who are same in substance, equal in power and glory. But we should note that in the Scriptures, the nomenclature "Father" does not only refer to the first person of the Trinity but also to the one living and true Triune God. In fact, it is often hard to decide with certainty whether an occurrence of the word actually refers to one or the other. Indeed, perhaps except for instances where it is very clear, such as Matthew 28:19, a good way of looking at it is that it refers to both. And it is no contradiction to do so for the Father is God, and God is Triune. Thus, for example, when the Lord Jesus teaches us to pray to the Father in the Lord's Prayer, He is actually teaching us to pray to God Triune, but at the same time, we should direct our prayer to the first person of the Godhead. So when we think of the first person of the Godhead, we must never conceive of Him as having a separate existence from the second and third persons of the Godhead.

This is how we must understand the first article of the Apostles' Creed. We believe that there is only one God, the Father Almighty, Creator of the heaven and earth. It is remarkable that no verse in the Scriptures directly attributes Creation to the First Person of the Trinity. We can find verses attributing Creation to the Son (e.g. Heb 2:1, 3; Eph 3:9; Col 1:16) and to the Spirit (e.g. Gen 1:2; Ps 104:30). But all other references to Creation attribute it to God Triune or to all persons of the Trinity without directly referring to the Father. Why then do we, together with all Christians, attribute Creation to the Father? The simple reason is that we understand with all Christians that when the Scripture refers to God without any qualification, we must think of the Father; and likewise, when the Scripture refers to the Father, we should think also of the Trinity and not just the first person of the Godhead (unlike in the case for the Second and Third Persons). This is why the Scripture speaks of God as our Father and of us as His sons and daughters (Mt 5:16, 45, 48; 1Jn 3:1-2 etc). With this in mind, we see how the Scripture leads us to attribute the creation of the heavens and the earth to God our Father in a multitude of verses (e.g. Gen 1:1; 2:4; Ex 20:11; 31:17; 2Kgs 19:15; 2Chr 2:12; Neh 9:6; Ps 115:15; 121:2; 124:8; Isa 42:5; Isa 45:12, 18; cf. v. 10; Jer 32:17; Jer 51:15; Acts 4:24; Acts 17:24; Rev 14:7; etc). Before Creation, nothing exists but God. In the fullness of time, Almighty God our Father created the heaven and the earth. That is to say, He made all things, visible and invisible, physical and spiritual. Even heaven is a created place. God our

Father made everything in the space of six days, "And God saw everything that He had made, and, behold, it was very good" (Gen 1:31). God our Father then governs all things by His sovereign power for His glory and for the sake of His children whom He made in His own image (cf. Acts 17:23).

Article II:
Of the Lord Jesus Christ

And [I believe] in Jesus Christ, His only begotten Son, our Lord;

Comments

The Apostle's Creed rightly begins with the First Person of the Trinity. We can't really begin to talk about the Lord Jesus Christ without first mentioning God the Father. But the heart of the Christian faith and confession is really the Lord Jesus Christ. This is why we are called Christian. We are Christian because we believe in Jesus Christ. Therefore, any articulation of faith without a central reference to the Lord Jesus Christ would reveal glaringly that the confessor is not truly Christian. Covenant children who grow up in an environment where the name of Christ is rightly mentioned routinely must especially be careful that they do not take for granted that they know Christ and therefore think nothing of speaking about Him as they talk about "believing in God." Although the Lord Jesus Christ is truly and fully God, parents of covenant children must make it a point to emphasise that when speaking of the person and work of the Lord Jesus Christ, we are referring to the God-Man and not exactly to God Triune.

Who exactly is the Lord Jesus Christ? In the next five articles of the Creed, we would be given to confess what we believe about Him that gives rise to the Christian faith. But for now, it is essential for us to make sure that we truly understand and appreciate every word we confess in this second article.

First of all, therefore, let us understand that the name "Jesus" is not just a name. It was indeed a common name in Palestine in the first century. But when this name is directly assigned by God Almighty to He whom we confess, we know that it is essential for us to know why the name is chosen. The fact is, the name "Jesus" means "Jehovah is salvation" or "Jehovah saves." He is so named, "for He shall save His people from their sins" (Mt 1:21). So when we take the name Jesus in our lips our heart must respond with grateful love towards He who is our Saviour.

Secondly, let us understand that "Christ," is not our Saviour's surname. Rather, it is His title. "Christ" is really the Greek equivalent of the Hebrew "Messiah" which means "Anointed One." Jesus Christ is the long-expected Messiah of Israel, the covenant people of God in the Old Testament. When we acknowledge Him as the Christ, we are identifying ourselves with the Israelites of old, and affirming the importance of knowing what the Old Testament teaches about Him.

Thirdly, in confessing that Christ Jesus is the "only begotten Son" of God, the Father Almighty, we are acknowledging His eternal sonship. In other words, we are confessing that He is fully and eternally God, one in essence with the Father, begotten, not made.

But fourthly, we are given to confess that He is "our Lord."

When the apostles called Christ "Lord" (Grk. *Κύριος, Kurios*) they were no doubt conscious of the fact that they were using a term which was used in the Greek Septuagint to translate the Hebrew Yahweh or Jehovah (e.g. cf. Joel 2:32; Rom 10:13). Thus the early Christian creed "Jesus is Lord" (Rom 10:9; 1 Cor 12:3; 2 Cor 2:5; Phil 2:11) is really an acknowledgement of the deity of Christ. Nevertheless, when we confess Jesus as "our Lord," we are not only affirming His deity but confessing our faith in Him and His Lordship over us. By living, suffering and dying for us, Christ has purchased us to Himself. And as such, we must respond with gratitude, love, loyalty, obedience and trust.

Article III:
Of the Conception & Birth of Christ

[I believe in Jesus Christ]
Who was conceived by the Holy Ghost, born of the virgin Mary;

Comments

The doctrine of the virgin birth of Jesus Christ is widely understood as one of the fundamentals of the faith that divides between biblical Christianity and Liberalism. John Gresham Machen is surely right that Liberalism is not Christianity. Today, there are many who would call themselves Christian, who do not believe in the virgin conception and birth of Christ. But the inclusion of the doctrine in the Apostles' Creed reflects the Christian consensus that no one could be a Christian in the biblical and historical sense of the word who does not believe in the virgin birth of Christ.

The doctrine is clearly taught in Scripture and is also theologically significant.

It was first prophesied in Isaiah 7:14—

"Therefore the Lord Himself shall give you a sign; Behold, a virgin shall conceive, and bear a son, and shall call His name Immanuel."

There are a variety of interpretations in regard to who the virgin in view was when the prophet Isaiah first spoke it to king

Ahaz. Suffice to say that there is no indication that the Jews in Old Testament days generally understood this verse as being a prophecy about the birth of the Messiah. But the Holy Spirit clearly intended it to be so, for before Joseph even took Mary to be his wife, the angel of the Lord appeared unto him in a dream to inform him that the child that Mary was carrying was conceived by the power of the Holy Ghost in fulfilment of Isaiah's prophecy (Mt 1:20-23).

Mary would later have other children with Joseph, but it is clear that Jesus was not the child of Joseph. He was born of a virgin. Joseph who was a descendant of David was His adoptive father so that He had a legal right to the throne of David. But remarkably, in the genealogy of Jesus through Joseph recorded in Matthew 1, one of His ancestors is given as Jechonias (v. 11). This is the Coniah or Jehoiachin, the son Jehoiakim whom God had cursed saying, "no man of his seed shall prosper, sitting upon the throne of David" (Jer 22:30). Were the Lord Jesus the actual son of Joseph and therefore the seed of Jechonias, He would have been disqualified from the throne. But lest any dispute the legitimacy of Jesus' claim to the throne, it should be noted that Mary also descended from David, only that her genealogy recorded in Luke 4, traces back to David through Nathan rather than Solomon (Lk 4:31), and therefore bypassing the cursed line altogether.

In any case, by confessing His virgin birth, we are acknowledging that the Lord Jesus is fully human. He was not injected into history with a temporary body. He shares our nature and has His own body, which grew from conception to maturity like all men. He is as such fit to be our representative (cf. Heb 2:14-17).

Theologically, it is essential that the Lord Jesus be born of a virgin for otherwise He would be of the seed of Adam and therefore guilty in him. By being born of a virgin, the Lord Jesus partook of our nature without being of the seed of Adam, and therefore was not federally imputed with his guilt (cf. Heb 7:9, 10). Therefore while He inherited His human nature from Mary, He did not inherit her corruption. More specifically, Mary was overshadowed by the power of the Holy Spirit (Lk 1:35), and Jesus was on the basis of His not being of the seed of Adam kept from inheriting her sinful nature. Thus the angel said unto her: "therefore also that holy thing which shall be born of thee shall be called the Son of God" (Lk 1:35).

Article IV:
Of the Suffering & Death of Christ

[I believe in Jesus Christ who]
Suffered under Pontius Pilate; was crucified, dead, and buried:
He descended into hell;

Comments

In the previous article, we were given to confess the virgin birth of Christ. In the present, we are immediately brought to His death. Rather curiously, the Creed appears to bypass the entire earthly life of our Lord. The Genevan Catechism of 1541 suggests that the reason for this leap is that the Creed highlights only "what pertains properly to the substance of our redemption." The Heidelberg Catechism, on the other hand, takes the word "suffered" somewhat out of context and suggests that it is a reference to the fact that Christ suffered "all the time that He lived on earth, but especially at the end of His life." Perhaps both opinions have merit, for it appears on surface reading that indeed the life of Christ is bypassed; but yet we know that the sufferings of Christ in His life (in what may be known as His preceptive or active obedience) is not insignificant at all (cf. Isa 53:3). Nevertheless, all of our Lord's suffering in His life find their significance ultimately in the Cross. Had there been no Cross, the lifetime of suffering would have little meaning. Thus it is conceivable that the original framers of the creed, in the interest of brevity has chosen to comprehend all of our Saviour's suffering under its climax at the Cross.

With this in mind, let us consider the 5 sub-points that we are given to confess in this article.

First of all, Christ Jesus *"suffered under Pontius Pilate."* Christ Jesus is altogether holy and without sin, and therefore He needs not to suffer. Yet He did. Why did He suffer? He suffered in order to pay for the penalty due to our sin. The prophet Isaiah puts this verity across most beautifully when he says:

"⁵ But He was wounded for our transgressions, He was bruised for our iniquities: the chastisement of our peace was upon Him; and with His stripes we are healed. ⁶ All we like sheep have gone astray; we have turned every one to his own way; and the LORD hath laid on Him the iniquity of us all" (Isa 53:5-6).

But why is the name of Pilate, as it were, immortalised in the Creed? Pilate was a wicked man whose fame or rather notoriety is closely connected to his wicked deed of crucifying the Lord rather than with any other accomplishments. Why then do we enunciate his name in this creed? We do so because first of all, it makes it clear that our Lord's death was clearly founded in history—for Pilate was governor in Judea in AD 26-36. But secondly, we do so because it reminds us of the innocence of our Lord since Pilate, as judge, had announced repeatedly that he found no fault with our Saviour (Jn 18:38;

19:4, 6).

But now, secondly, we are given to confess that Christ Jesus *"was crucified."* This, of course, speaks of the manner in which our Lord was executed. Why is it important for us to confess that He was crucified? We can think of several reasons such as the prophecies which clearly pointed to the Lord's death on the cross (e.g. Psalm 22:16-17). But the most important reason why Christ had to die on the Cross is that the death on the cross is a cursed death. So when we confess that He was crucified, we are confessing that He died in order to redeem us "from the curse of the law, being made a curse for us: for it is written, Cursed is every one that hangeth on a tree" (Gal 3:13). The Cross, therefore, speaks of the substitutionary atonement of Christ on our behalf.

In the third place, we are given to confess that Christ Jesus was *"dead."* By this single word, we are acknowledging that Christ paid for our sin fully, for the wages of sin is death (Rom 6:23). He died physically so as to redeem us from physical death. He experienced spiritual death when in the three hours of darkness He endured the wrath of God on our behalf. The pains of hell is simply to experience the wrath of an angry God (Heb 10:31). So painful was the torment that our Lord exclaimed at the end of the three hours, "My God, my God, why hast thou forsaken me?" (Mt 27:46). All through His earthly ministry, Christ had addressed His Father as "Father," but now because He was bearing our sin, and was being *punished* and receiving the wages for our sin, His sense of familial fellowship was momentarily overwhelmed.

In the fourth place, we are given to confess that Christ Jesus our Lord was *"buried."* By this, we are affirming that He did really die bodily contrary to some unbelieving theories that He might have just fainted etc. Our Lord did not only die. He was pierced in His side to make sure He was really dead (Jn 19:34); and then He was prepared for burial according to the Jewish custom with "a mixture of myrrh and aloes, about an hundred pound weight" (Jn 19:39).

Then He was buried in the tomb belonging to Joseph of Arimathea, "which he had hewn out in the rock" and a great stone was rolled over its entrance to secure it (Mt 27:60). Our Lord had to die if He were to conquer death for us. Thus, He did and He was buried so that we may have no doubt that He died; and so that we may have no doubt that He rose from the dead for our justification (Rom 4:25).

Finally, we are given to confess that "He descended into hell." As we noted in our introductory article on the creed as a whole, this phrase was a late inclusion. Nevertheless, since it is in the version of the creed that most modern believers are familiar with, it is right that we use it, but with a right understanding. In this regard, given that the phrase *follows* the reference to the Lord's burial, the *Westminster Larger Catechism* is probably right that it should be taken as a reference to Christ being "under the power of death till the third day" (WLC 50). This was so not only to fulfil prophecy (cf. Mt 12:40), but also to bring us to the eighth day, or to the first day of the new week. Christ would rise on the first day of the new week to indicate a new beginning for His Church.

Article V:
Of the Resurrection of Christ

[I believe in Jesus Christ who suffered and died for us that]
The third day He arose again from the dead

Comments

The resurrection of Christ is undoubtedly a fundamental and central verity of the Christian Faith. The apostle Paul includes it as a basic proposition of the gospel along with the propitiatory death of Christ (1 Cor 15:4); and he tells us that "if Christ be not risen, then is our preaching vain, and [our] faith is also vain" (1 Cor 15:14).

Indeed, so central is the resurrection to the Christian faith that Luke could speak of "the resurrection of the Lord Jesus" as a synonym of the gospel (Acts 4:33). Indeed, Paul even appears to distil saving faith and the confession thereof to just one fact that "God hath raised [the Lord Jesus] from the dead" (Rom 10:9)!

Why is the resurrection so important? It is important because if Christ did not rise from the dead, then we can have no assurance that His death was sufficient to pay for our sin! When Paul says, the Lord "was raised again for our justification" (Rom 4:25), he is clearly indicating that He rose because there is no just reason to keep Him in the grave since He has paid sufficiently for our sin. Similarly, we can expect to be raised at the Last Day only because Christ who is united to us was raised as the firstfruit of all who died in faith (1Cor 15:20).

These biblical observations and assertions lead us to the inevitable conclusion that the gospel would cease to be gospel void of the resurrection and that no professing believers can deny the resurrection of Christ and still be regarded as Christian.

Indeed, although faith is required to hold on to the doctrine, it is not a blind faith, for the biblical evidence for it is insurmountable whereas the objections are easily answered.

We need not answer those who do not believe in the resurrection of Christ just because they do not believe in anything supernatural anyway. But for those who claim they do not believe because of apparent contradictions between the various accounts and Paul's presentation of it, we answer first of all that if it was a fraud, those who were responsible for perpetuating it would surely have been more careful to paint a consistent picture. That said, we must insist that there are no real contradictions between the gospel accounts. All the apparent discrepancies can be easily reconciled without forcing any unintended meaning to the statements in the accounts.[1]

---

[1] For example, John appears to put Mary Magdalene's encounter with the angels after Peter and John went to the tomb (Jn 20:10-12), whereas Luke puts it as before (Lk 24:4-12). How do we reconcile the 'discrepancy'? Well, actually, if you read the account of Luke and the account of John carefully, you will realize that Luke and John are in fact describing two different encounters with the angels—the first (of Matthew, Mark and Luke) involving the women who went with Mary Magdalene, whereas the other

What about the fact that the apostle Paul makes no mention of the Lord meeting the women, but spoke of Him as appearing to Peter first? Well, the simple answer to that would be that Paul was seeking to persuade anyone still not convinced that the resurrection did actually take place. This being so, it would make sense for him to cite only witnesses who were generally accepted, and it is a fact that women were not regarded by the Jews as legally credible witnesses.

But is there any evidence to confirm that the resurrection of the Lord did actually take place? Well, there are no external scientific and empirical evidence that may conclusively prove it. But if the Gospel and ecclesiastical accounts are to be admitted (and there is no compelling reason not to admit them), then there are several rational proofs that go beyond the bare statements of assertions.

We think firstly of the historical record of the Lord Jesus appearing to the women first (Mk 16:9; Mt 28:9-10). As we mentioned, the testimony of women was generally not accepted by the Jews. Were the accounts of the resurrection fabricated, it would have been far more credible had it been reported that *men*

---

involving Mary Magdalene only! John simply left out mentioning the first encounter whereas Luke records the first encounter. What appears to have happened is that when Mary arrived at the sepulchre with her companions, she saw that the stone was rolled away, noticed that the Lord's body was not in the tomb and immediately ran off to tell Peter and John (Jn 20:1-2). The other women entered the sepulchre without her and there met the angels who spoke to them (Lk 24:4-5). After they left (Mk 16:8), Peter and John arrived at the Sepulchre. Mary finally came back to the sepulchre, by which time Peter and John had also left (Jn 20:10). It was then that Mary encountered the angels and then the Lord Himself (Jn 20:11-17).

rather than women saw Him first.

Secondly, we think of how the Jewish and Roman authorities never produced any evidence to back up their claim that the disciples of the Lord stole the Lord's body. We would imagine how they would have given that top priority for their reputation and credibility was at stake—unless of course, they understood that the more they tried to bolster their false assertion, the more the truth would be strengthened.

Thirdly, we note how the Church began to worship on the first day of the week so quickly after the death of the Lord, when the Lord Himself worshipped on the sixth day. This indicates that the church must have unanimously understood that the Christ had changed the day dramatically. What better way for Him to do so than by the resurrection. "The stone which the builders refused is become the head stone of the corner. This is the day which the LORD hath made; we will rejoice and be glad in it" (Ps 118:22, 24).

Fourthly, we see how the disciples were transformed dramatically from being very timid and doubtful to those who were brave and resolute in their conviction. Nothing short of assurance of the Lord's resurrection could have made that change. Had they been complicit in fraud, we can imagine how they would be weakened rather than strengthened in their ministry.

Fifthly, we see how the apostle Paul invited open enquiries and objections when he indicated to the Corinthians Church that there were five hundred witnesses of the Lord's resurrection, of whom the greater part remained alive (1 Cor 15:6). That was around AD 55, and it is clear from the way that Paul dealt with the subject that there were already many sceptics who did not believe that Christ rose from the dead. Paul's claim could easily have been challenged and refuted by these had it been false. So the universal acceptance by the churches of his claims as authentic goes a long way to demonstrate its veracity.

Finally, we must not forget the change that happened to Paul. Paul was clearly an intellectual man of strict morals as his letters indicate. Yet, from one who persecuted the church out of conviction, he became a champion of the faith. Paul must have been first convicted of the truth and converted.

Thus we firmly believe that Christ did indeed rise from the dead, and our belief is not irrational and based on bare assertions.

Of the Ascension of Christ

[I believe in Jesus Christ who suffered, died and rose for us that]
He ascended into heaven,
and sitteth at the right hand of God the Father Almighty

Comments

If the resurrection of Christ is a foundational truth of the Christian faith, the ascension and session of Christ are unifying truths. If Christ had not risen from the dead, our faith is vain and we are yet in our sin. If Christ had not ascended to heaven and is seated at the right hand of God the Father, then our faith is powerless and we are without hope.

The ascension of Christ was prophesied in the Old Testament in passages such as Psalm 68:18 (cf. Eph 4:8) and Daniel 7:13 (cf. Acts 1:9). The fulfilment of these prophesies occurred forty days after He rose from the dead (Acts 1:3). Luke, in particular, tells us that that the Lord led His disciples out as far as Bethany or the Mount of Olives (Lk 24:50). Then, after He given them some final instruction and blessing them, He was "taken up, and a cloud received Him out of their sight" (Acts 1:9; Lk 24:51).

Where Luke leaves off, the prophecy of Daniel takes over and we are told:

"I saw in the night visions, and, behold, one like the Son of man came with the clouds of heaven, and came to the Ancient of days, and they brought Him near before Him" (Dan 7:13).

And thus begins the session of the Lord Jesus Christ at the right hand of the throne of God.

The apostle to the Hebrews tells us that Christ Jesus,…

"[3] Who being the brightness of His glory, and the express image of His person, and upholding all things by the word of His power, when He had by Himself purged our sins, sat down on the right hand of the Majesty on high…" (Heb 1:1-3; cf. Heb 12:2).

What is it to sit on the right hand of the Majesty on high? Clearly, this is not intended to be taken literally since "God is a spirit" (Jn 4:24), so He does not have a locality, much less a throne to sit on. Thus, the language must be understood metaphorically, no doubt, to express the exalted position of power and authority of Christ as the God-Man. Thus we are told in 1 Peter 3:22 that Jesus "is gone into heaven, and is on the right hand of God; angels and authorities and powers being made subject unto Him."

This is a picture borrowed from the fact that in Eastern and Near Eastern courts, the most powerful man beside the king is given a seat on the right hand, the right hand being recognised as the hand of power and authority.

What is the significance of our Lord's sitting at the right hand of

God? What is He doing in that exalted position?

In the first place, He has, no doubt, been appointed a ruler and governor over all. He is upholding all things by the word of His power for the sake of His church (Heb 1:3), and working all thing for the good of His people even as He awaits the consummation of His reign. This was prophesied in Psalm 110:1 and quoted numerous times in the New Testament:

> "The LORD said unto my Lord, Sit thou at my right hand, until I make thine enemies thy footstool" (Ps 110:1; cf. Mt 22:44).

Our Lord would remain in that position of power until the last of the elect is brought in and the world is ripe for final judgement, at which time, He would return as Victorious King and Judge.

But secondly, He is seated at the right hand of God in order to function as our Great High Priest, to make intercession for us (Heb 8:1; Rom 8:34). On what basis does He make intercession for us? He makes it on the basis of His sacrifice on our behalf. This is alluded to in Hebrews 10:12 where are told, "this man, after He had offered one sacrifice for sins for ever, sat down on the right hand of God." The Old Testament priests could only make intercession by daily sacrifices; Christ, on the other hand, offered one sacrifice, and from then on continued as our intercessor on the basis of that all-sufficient sacrifice.

Thirdly and finally, the ascended Christ is preparing an eternal dwelling place for us in His position of authority. He said to His disciples: "In my Father's house are many mansions: if it were not so, I would have told you. I go to prepare a place for you" (Jn 14:2).

It is with this hope and assurance, that we confess that Jesus *"ascended into heaven, and sitteth at the right hand of God the Father Almighty."* Amen.

Article VII:
Of the Second Coming of Christ

[I believe in Jesus Christ who suffered, died and rose for us before ascending into heaven and sitting at the right hand of God, that...]

From thence He shall come to judge the quick and the dead

Comments

Hitherto, the statements in the Creed about the work of Christ have been framed in the past tense because they concern things that have already occurred. In the present article, however, we are looking at things future and thus we have a statement framed in the future tense.

Christ has arisen, is ascended and is seated at the right hand of the throne of God as the governor of the universe and our intercessor. But this is not the end of what He will do for us, for the Scripture teaches us that He will come again. The apostle Peter has made it clear that "the heaven must receive [Jesus Christ] until the times of the restitution of all things" (Acts 3:21). Christ will return from heaven at the day of the restitution of all things. This day is known in Scriptures as the "last day" whereas the days between the first and second comings of Christ is known as the "last days" (Heb 12:1; 2 Tim 3:1). The Last Day is the day of the general resurrection (Jn 11:24; etc) when both of the just and the unjust will be raised

28

(Acts 24:1). It is also the day of the general judgement (Jn 12:48) when both believers (i.e. "the quick") and unbelievers (i.e. "the dead") will face a public judgement and then ushered into their eternal abode (Acts 10:42; 2 Tim 4:1; Mt 25:46).

How will Christ Jesus return? What will happen then?

Firstly, the angels who attended His ascension said at that time, "this same Jesus, which is taken up from you into heaven, shall so come in like manner as ye have seen Him go into heaven" (Acts 1:11). In other words, His return will involve a corporal and visible descend.

Secondly, the Lord Himself indicates that He will come "in the clouds of heaven with power and great glory" (Mt 24:30; cf. Lk 9:26) with "all the holy angels with Him" (Mt 25:31).

Thirdly, the apostle Paul reminds us that "the Lord Himself shall descend from heaven with a shout, with the voice of the archangel, and with the trump of God" (1 Th 4:16). It will obviously be a very public rather than a secret event.

Fourthly, Paul tells us that as the Lord descends, "the dead in Christ shall rise first: Then we which are alive and remain shall be caught up together with them in the clouds, to meet the Lord in the air" (1 Th 4:16-17).

Fifthly, we may infer that we shall all descend with the Lord for the rest of our journey to the earth. We infer this from the fact that the word translated "to meet" (Grk. ἀπάντησις, *apantēsis*) in 1 Thessalonians 4:17 is always translated in Scripture to speak of meeting someone to escort him for the remainder of his journey. It is thus used of the wise virgins who go out to meet the bridegroom (Mt 25:1, 6); and also of the friends of Paul from Rome who went as far as Appii forum to meet Paul as he arrived at Rome (Acts 28:15).

Sixthly, we infer that in the meantime, the reprobate will also be raised or changed (cf. Dan 12:2). While the elect will put on an incorruptible and glorious body, the reprobate will put on a perpetually corruptible and contemptible body.

Finally, the Lord will sit upon a Seat of Judgement, the whole multitude of all people who ever lived will stand before Him to be judged (Acts 17:31; Mt 25:32ff). The elect will be gathered on His right whereas the reprobate will be gathered on His left. This division prior to the beginning of the judicial process indicates that the eternal destiny of those being judged is not determined by their works. Nevertheless, it is clear that all who are saved are given grace to do good works, for which they engage in willingly without any thought as to whether it is worthwhile and profitable for them. They give "cups of cold water" (cf. Mt 10:42; 25:36) simply because they are created in Christ Jesus unto good works (Eph 2:10) so that doing good works out of love and gratitude towards Christ became part of their nature. These, imputed with righteousness and proven to be righteous, will be ushered "into life eternal" whereas the reprobates, who will also prove themselves to be unrighteous "shall go away into everlasting punishment" (Mt 25:46).

Article VIII:
Of the Holy Spirit

I believe in the Holy Ghost

Comments

The Christian Faith is Trinitarian. We believe that there is but one living and true God. But we also believe that there are three persons in the Godhead: the Father, the Son and the Holy Ghost, and these three are one God, same in substance, equal in power and glory. Therefore everyone who truly believes in Christ Jesus and confesses Him as Lord and Saviour will also believe in the Holy Ghost. Or to put it in another way, biblical and historical Christianity does not accept as Christian those not believe in the Holy Ghost as taught in the Word of God.

In particular, we believe that the Holy Ghost or the Holy Spirit is the Second Person of the Trinity. He is not the Father, He is not the Son, but He is God. He is not a force or an influence. He is a divine person just as the Father and the Son are divine persons. He is co-eternal, co-substantial and co-equal with the Father and the Son, and He enjoys perfect communication with them.

Conversely, do not accept as brethren in Christ anyone who claims to be Christian, but do not believe the Holy Spirit is a divine Person distinct from the Father and the Son.

More specifically, we reject as Christians, those who hold to all

31

forms of anti-Trinitarian Monotheism (e.g. of Judaism or Islam); of Unitarianism (one God in one Person); of Modalism (one God manifested in three modes, e.g. in Oneness Pentecostalism); of Binitarianism (one God in two Persons, the Father and Christ); and Social Trinitarianism or Tritheism (three Persons or three Gods united by mutual love and accord).

But what do we believe about the Holy Spirit? We believe He was involved: (1) in the Creation of the Universe (Gen 1:2); (2) in the prophetic revelations about Christ in Old Testament days (1Pt 1:11); (3) in the Lord Jesus' miraculous conception (Mt 1:20); (4) in the anointing of Christ (Lk 3:22; Lk 4:18);[2] (5) in the resurrection of Christ (Rom 8:11); (6) in the great outpouring of power and the establishment of the New Testament Church at Pentecost (Acts 2:1ff); and (7) the inspiration of Holy Scripture (2 Tim 3:16).

The Holy Spirit has not ceased to work. He continues to work powerfully in the Church and in the hearts of the elect. For examples: (1) as the "Spirit of Life" (Rom 8:2), He quickens and regenerates (Jn 6:63; Tit 3:5); (2) as the "Spirit of Adoption," He indwells us and gives us the freedom to walk as the children of God (cf. Rom 8:1; 2 Cor 3:17); (3) as the "Spirit of faith" (2Cor 4:13), He enables us to believe unto salvation (Eph 2:8); (4) as the "Spirit of Truth" (Jn 14:17) and as the "Comforter", He dwells in us to illumine our minds in the truth and to bring to

---

[2] The word "Christ" comes from the Greek Christos, which is equivalent of the Hebrew, "Messiah," which means "Anointed One"

remembrance whatsoever Christ has said to us through preaching and through our reading of the Scriptures (Jn 14:26); (5) as "the Spirit of Grace" (Heb 10:29), He works in us to sanctify us so that we grow in righteousness (2Th 2:13; Phil 2:13); (6) as "the Spirit of Christ" (Rom 8:9), He produces the Fruit of the Spirit in us (Gal 5:22-23) so that we grow in Christ-likeness and joy in Christ (Rom 14:17); and finally, (7) as the "Spirit of Promise" (Eph 1:13), He seals our salvation and gives us hope as "the earnest of our inheritance unto the redemption of the purchase possession" (Eph 1:14).

A large segment of the modern church, perhaps in its zeal to restore the Holy Spirit to His rightful place in the life of the Church and the Christian has veered into mysticism, superstition and falsehood. The Holy Spirit is not something or someone we can make use of or exploit. Neither does the Holy Spirit today give us new revelation as some claim. Nevertheless, it is important for us to understand that no true believer can truly walk as a believer without the work of the Holy Spirit in His heart. Faith is a gift of God wrought by the Holy Spirit in our heart. The Spirit dwells in the heart of all who have true faith. And if the Holy Spirit dwells in our heart, He will work to sanctify us; and we will grow spiritually and we will bear spiritual fruit that makes us more and more like Christ the only begotten of the Father. If this is not happening, then it is likely that we have not begun to walk with Christ. If we have not begun to walk with Christ, we are not truly Christ. The Christian believes in the Holy Spirit and is led by Him.

Article IX:
Of the Church Universal

I believe an holy catholic church: the communion of saints

Comments

One of the purposes of the Apostles' Creed is so that believers may have a statement to confess their faith with one voice and a banner to walk and worship together in unity of faith. This body of believers is known as the "church." The church, according to the scriptural usage of the term, refers to the congregation of people who are called out of the world and received by God as the body of Christ. The head of the church, as such, is Christ (cf. Eph 5:23).

From this basic and general understanding of the church, however, we must grasp the idea that the church can be viewed from different perspectives and distinctions.

In particular, there is an aspect of the church that is invisible and another that is visible. The church invisible comprises all the elect of Christ throughout the ages. These are true members of the church of Christ for whom Christ laid His life down for (Eph 5:25). Membership in the church invisible is ratified by Baptism of the Holy Spirit or regeneration. The church visible, on the other hand, comprises credibly-professing believers and their children upon the earth at any one time. Membership in the church visible is ratified by water baptism (cf. Acts 2:47).

There is, moreover, a geographic dimension to the church visible that should be noted, for there is such a thing as a church local (e.g. Acts 9:31; 15:41; Acts 16:5; 1 Cor 14:33, etc) and a church universal (e.g. 1Cor 12:28). When an ordinary member of the church refers to the church he is most likely to be referring to the church local visible. However, it is necessary for us to believe in the church universal.

This is why we are given to confess, "*I believe an holy catholic church.*"

The term 'holy' speaks of how the church is set apart unto God. It must be viewed indicatively to declare what we are, and imperatively to speak of what we ought to be. The church is holy because her members are redeemed by Christ, covered in His righteousness and sanctified by the Holy Spirit. Thus she must seek to be holy as God is holy. She must function in the way that Christ has dictated in His Word that she may remain as the salt and light in the world. She must not allow herself to conform unto the world by adopting worldly methods and principles.

The term 'catholic', on the other hand, speaks of the universality of the church. It has nothing to do with the Roman Catholic Church (which is a contradiction of terms and which is not truly Christian and therefore not truly a part of the church). It speaks rather of how Christ has purchased only one church. All true believers are members of this church. We are members of the church universal invisible by election. We are in the same church as Noah, Moses, David, Isaiah, Athanasius, Augustine, Luther, Calvin, Knox, Edwards, etc. Our elect children and children's children down the generations are members of this same church. But there is also a sense in which we are members of the church universal visible. Christ prayed in His high priestly prayer of His desire that the church may be one (Jn 17:11 etc). The church universal invisible is already one by definition. So, the Lord's prayer must relate to the church universal visible. It speaks of Christ's desire, and our duty to work on Christian unity.

So there is an indicative and an imperative sense to the word 'catholic' as in the case for the word 'holy.' It is the duty of the church to seek to be united in biblical and confessional truth rather than separated by geography, race, culture, politics, nationality, social status, age, background, etc.

Moreover, in confessing our belief in the holy catholic church, we are acknowledging our obligation to remain in her and to serve the Lord within her. Therefore, we are given also to confess that we believe in *"the communion of saints."* The term *'saints'* means 'holy ones.' All believers are 'holy ones' (cf. Rom 1:7; 1Cor 1:2 etc). As believers, we are all in common members of Christ and partakers of His gifts and riches (Rom 8:32). We are one because we are united to Christ and are joined together by His providence and by His Spirit (1 Cor 12:13). Therefore, it behoves us to cultivate fellowship with one another by employing our gifts and riches for the advantage and salvation of each other in the church (Phil 2:4-6; 1 Jn 1:3-4). This we confess to be our duty and privilege as those who are redeemed by the blood of Christ joined together with members of His church by His wisdom and providence. Amen.

Article X:
Of Forgiveness of Sins

[I believe in]

The forgiveness of sins

Comments

Forgiveness is a central theme in Christianity. Indeed the church is essentially a congregation of sinners, saved by grace, forgiven of God the Father, justified by God the Son and freed from the sense of guilt by the work of God the Spirit.

Believers have need of forgiveness and need to forgive.

We are debtors to God because of our sin. But our sins have been paid for, and we were forgiven. How was our sin paid for? The scripture reveals that the wages of sin is death, even death physical, spiritual and eternal (cf. Rom 6:23). Therefore the payment for our sin must involve death. Either we must suffer death for all eternity for our sin against an infinite God, or another must suffer death for us. Thank God that our sins were paid for by another. But how could it be just if our sin were paid for by another who never sinned? And how could there be forgiveness if God required payment from another? Well, technically, if God does not pursue our debt because someone paid for our debt, then we may be said to be forgiven of our debt. However, we have not really been lovingly forgiven. We have simply cleared our debt. Such a forgiveness does not give rise to a loving response.

Suppose someone owes you a million dollars and a good friend of his comes to you to pay his debt on his behalf. You, having received the money, will not pursue the debt. But have you really forgiven the debtor in such a way as to invoke love? No, you are simply relating to him legally as one who does not owe you anything anymore. If you would truly and lovingly forgive the debtor, you must suffer loss by writing off the debt. Loving forgiveness will always cost something. In this case, to forgive, you must, as it were, pay the debt out of your own pocket!

Thankfully, this was what God did for us. God could not simply overlook the sin, for that would be an injustice. Christ is appointed to pay for our sin, and remarkably Christ is not a third party. Were He a third party, it would be unjust for God to punish Him for our sin; and God would not have truly forgiven us. The fact is that Christ, as the Second Person of Triune God, is really the aggrieved party. By having Christ to receive our punishment on our behalf, God is essentially suffering loss on our behalf. Therefore, we can say that God has forgiven us!

Of course, until the Spirit opened our eyes, we did not know that Christ has already paid for our sin. We continue to sin against God and therefore incur God's wrath daily. Thus we are "by nature the children of wrath, even as others" (Eph 2:3). But when we are quickened and receive Christ as our Lord and Saviour, we are at the same time made cognisant to the fact that we are beloved and forgiven of our sin. We may call this a judicial forgiveness, for although it involves a loving cancellation of our debt, we are given an emphasis that God will not pursue payment because Christ has already paid for our debt. Thus Paul reminds us: "There is therefore now no condemnation to them which are in Christ Jesus..." (Rom 8:1).

But this is not the only forgiveness we need, for the Lord Jesus teaches us to pray in the fifth petition of the Lord's Prayer: "Forgive us our debts, as we forgive our debtors" (Mt 6:12). Why do we need to seek God's forgiveness if we are already forgiven? We need to do so because sin estranges us from God so that we incur God's fatherly displeasure. "If I regard iniquity in my heart, the Lord will not hear me" says the Psalmist (Ps 66:18). A child will always be beloved by his father, but the father may be angered by the child's transgression and refuse to show him his love until the child seeks his forgiveness. This is so with our heavenly Father. Thus, we must daily seek our Father's forgiveness for our sins.

Moreover, as our Lord teaches us in the fifth petition, since we are a forgiven people, we must forgive one another. The Lord says: "When ye stand praying, forgive, if ye have ought against any... but if ye do not forgive, neither will your Father which is in heaven forgive your trespasses" (Mk 11:25-26). By these words, our Lord is essentially saying that no true believer who has been forgiven of his sin will refuse to forgive another who seeks his forgiveness. On the contrary, every believer who has been touched by the forgiveness of God will have a heart of forgiveness which is ever ready to forgive. It was with such a heart that our Lord cried on the Cross, "Father, forgive them; for they know not what they do" (Lk 23:34). Our Lord clearly believed in forgiveness, and so must we. Amen.

Article XI:
Of the Resurrection

[I believe in]

The resurrection of the body

Comments

We have already considered, in Article V, the Resurrection of the Lord Jesus Christ. All true believers will confess that Christ Jesus died for their sin and rose again from the dead on the third day. But those who believe in the resurrection of the Lord Jesus will also confess that they believe in "the resurrection of the body."

In the first place, we cannot confess that Christ Jesus rose from the dead bodily if we do not believe in the resurrection of the body. "If there be no resurrection of the dead, then is Christ not risen," says the apostle Paul (1 Cor 15:13).

Secondly, as the apostle Paul also asserts, "Christ [is] risen from the dead, and become the firstfruits of them that slept" (1 Cor 15:20). The fact is Christ did not rise from the dead as a private individual. Rather, rose from the dead as the covenant head of the elect just as He died for them as their covenant head. Since He rose, all who are united to Him will also rise one day because their bodies remain united to Him even when they are laid in the grave. Thus He declared to Martha:

"I am the resurrection, and the life: he that believeth in me, though he were dead, yet shall he live: And whosoever liveth and believeth in me shall never die. Believest thou this?" (Jn 11:25-26).

When will the resurrection occur? The Lord Himself says:

"And this is the will of Him that sent me, that every one which seeth the Son, and believeth on Him, may have everlasting life: and I will raise him up at the last day" (Jn 6:40).

The Last Day is, no doubt, the day that the Lord Jesus will return again as triumphal Judge and King. In that day, says the apostle Paul,

"The Lord Himself shall descend from heaven with a shout, with the voice of the archangel, and with the trump of God: and the dead in Christ shall rise first: Then we which are alive and remain shall be caught up together with them in the clouds, to meet the Lord in the air…" (1 Th 4:16-17).

How will the bodies be raised? The bodies of believers will be raised glorious and incorruptible—

"It is sown in corruption; it is raised in incorruption: [43] It is sown in dishonour; it is raised in glory: it is sown in weakness; it is raised in power: [44] It is sown a natural body; it is raised a spiritual body. There is a natural body, and there is a spiritual body" (1 Cor 15:43-44).

We believe that we will be raised with the self-same body with which we leave this present life. This, of course, does not mean that every molecule in our body when we die will be re-gathered. The fact is that we are never defined molecularly. Our molecular constitution is changing from moment to moment even as we breathe and eat and move. And some of our molecules with which we die would end up, at least temporarily in the bodies of other persons.

No, no; the body that is raised is related to the body that died in the manner that a plant that grows out of the ground is related to the seed that was sown. This is the point that Paul is teaching us by using an agricultural metaphor of sowing (Grk. σπείρω, speirō). And this is also the reason why the Church has traditionally practised burial rather than cremation for the dead. Cremation reminds us of judgement. Burial, on the other hand, bears testimony to our belief that one day there will emerge from the grave a glorious resurrected body.

But what about the unconverted? Will they be raised too? Clearly, they will be. The Lord Jesus Himself states:

"Marvel not at this: for the hour is coming, in the which all that are in the graves shall hear His voice, and shall come forth; they that have done good, unto the resurrection of life; and they that have done evil, unto the resurrection of damnation" (Jn 5:29; cf. Dan 12:2).

Believers will be raised incorruptible and glorious, never to suffer sicknesses, death, pain, sorrow and frustration. They will have a body that is adapted to glorifying God and enjoying God and His people for all eternity. On the other hand, unbelievers will be raised corruptible and contemptible, with a body that is adapted to experience to the fullest the torments and sorrows of the Lake of Fire for all eternity.

We believe these things because the Scripture teaches us the same. Amen.

Article XII:
Of Life Everlasting

And [I believe in] the life everlasting. AMEN.

Comments

Probably, the most famous verse in the Bible in the modern church is John 3:16—

> "For God so loved the world, that He gave His only begotten Son, that whosoever believeth in Him should not perish, but have everlasting life" (Jn 3:16).

While the interpretation of this verse,—especially as it pertains to the meaning of the word "world",—has given rise to some disagreements amongst believers, all are agreed that "everlasting life" or "eternal life" is God's gift to all who believe in the Lord Jesus Christ. The apostle Paul says:

> "For the wages of sin is death; but the gift of God is eternal life through Jesus Christ our Lord." (Rom 6:23)

All Christians believe in life everlasting.

But what exactly is life everlasting?

In the first place, life everlasting is obviously life that never ends. We believe that the human soul is held in immortal existence by the power of God. Even the reprobate will have an everlasting existence, but because their existence after life in this world is one of never-ending sorrow and pain, we do not call it everlasting life, but everlasting death. The elect in Christ, on the other hand, will live on forever and ever in a meaningful and joyous existence.

In the second place, this life that is everlasting is meaningful and joyous because it is a life of enjoying God. The Lord Jesus says in His high priestly prayer:

> "This is life eternal, that they might know thee the only true God, and Jesus Christ, whom thou hast sent" (Jn 17:3).

In other words, the essence of eternal life is not in its eternality, but in its fellowship with God the Father and God the Son.

In the third place, this everlasting life will be enjoyed fully only after the resurrection. Thus, David says:

> "Thou wilt shew me the path of life: in thy presence is fulness of joy; at thy right hand there are pleasures for evermore" (Ps 16:11).

It is clear from inspired commentary in Acts 2:25-28 that David is referring to the fulness of joy that comes with the resurrection.

This is also, no doubt, the reason why we are given in the Apostle Creed to confess that we believe in "everlasting life" only after we confess that we believe in the "resurrection of the body."

Christ came to redeem us in our body and soul. In this life, we are given a foretaste of our heavenly eternal life by the Spirit being given to dwell in us as an earnest of our eternal inheritance. When we leave this present life, our souls will be made perfect that we may enjoy spiritual fellowship with God. But it is only in the Last Day when our bodies are raised from the dead and reunited to our soul that we shall enjoy a life abundantly and joyous perfectly.

This is the hope of every believer as he runs to the Celestial City together with the whole company of fellow saints, all looking unto Jesus the Author and Finisher of their faith. Amen and Amen.

Index of Scripture